DILRAJ MANN

DALSTON MONSTERZZ

NOBROW

LONDON | NEW YORK

HUFF...
HUFF...
clack
clack
clack
clack
clack
RRAGH!!!
AAAAiiiEEEEE!!!!
RUBBISH!
BOO
BOOO
BOOOBOOO
BOOO
THAT BEAST IS GETTING SLOWER...
...WEAKER.
YOU NEED TO KEEP THIS EXCITING, OLD BOY.
DON'T FRET, BOWER.
WE HAVE A PLAN.

HOLLOWAY
PRISON AND
YOUTH OFFE

STILL WAITING?
YEAH.
WELL, STAY OUT OF TROUBLE, ROSHAN.
YOI

DON'T WANT TO SEE YOU HERE AGAIN.
I DON'T PLAN TO COME BACK, MR CARLIN.

6:45
HE'S LATE!

HEY, LEGO HEAD!

YOU NEED TO GET THAT MOP CUT, BRO.
YOU LOOK LIKE ONE OF THEM BEATLES.
THOUGHT YOU'D FORGOTTEN TODAY WAS THE DAY.

I HAD IT IN MY DIARY: ROSH ESCAPES.

THANKS, MAN.

NEW BIKE?
YES. YES.
JUST GOT TO DO A QUICK DELIVERY ON THE WAY HOME.

www.newzoo.com
NEWZOO
Another business man goes missing. And in other news, monsters are reportedly still being sighted in East London. Are they real?
News Sport Weather TV Radio

www.newzoo.com
NEWZOO
Members of the public repeatedly reported sightings of giant creatures in East London but no video footage has ever surfaced.
News Sport Weather TV Radio

www.newzoo.com
NEWZOO
Dalston Mill Fabrics
There's hordes of them running around at night. It's scary… I just wish it was the way it used to be.
News Sport Weather TV Radio
AND THEN THE GUY SAYS TO HIM 'YOU BETTER GIVE ME BACK MY BIKE OR I'LL POP YOU'.
BUT TOSH DIDN'T CARE AND BOMBED IT STRAIGHT INTO A CAR...

SO HE'S IN HOSPITAL. JIMMY GOT A GIRLFRIEND SO HE'S NOT AROUND...
SOUNDS LIKE I MISSED LOADS...
MOT
LET

BRRRRRMMMM!!

HEY
YOU RIPPED ME OFF!

THIS WEED IS PARSLEY!

MOVE IT!!

EEEEEEEEEEEEE

CHICKEN
WHY ARE YOU STOP—
OH.
Money Lin
PAL STOR
WHEN THE MONSTERS FIRST APPEARED, EVERYONE WAS PETRIFIED...

YOU'D SEE THEM IN THE MIDDLE OF THE NIGHT... EATING OUT OF BINS AND RUNNING THROUGH THE STREETS. HEAR THEM JUMPING ON ROOFTOPS AND SETTING OFF CAR ALARMS.
FOXES JUST DISAPPEARED OVERNIGHT.
LIKE WOODLICE FROM UNDER A ROCK, MONSTERS EMERGED FROM THE GROUND, STIRRED BY ARMIES OF DIGGERS RIPPING UP THE EARTH SO THAT NEW LUXURY FLATS COULD BE BUILT.

THEN SOME KID RODE ONE.
SOON LOTS OF KIDS — AND IT WAS ALWAYS KIDS — STARTED RIDING THEM.

TURNED OUT THE MONSTERS WERE PRETTY STUPID AND CRAZY TERRITORIAL.
THEY'D FIGHT OVER A CIRCLE DRAWN IN CHALK.

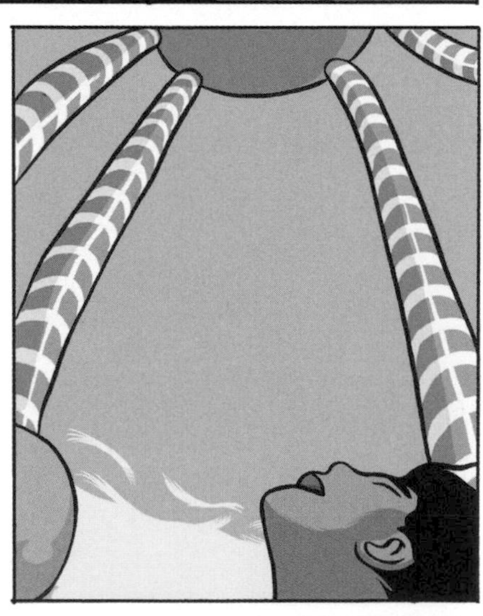

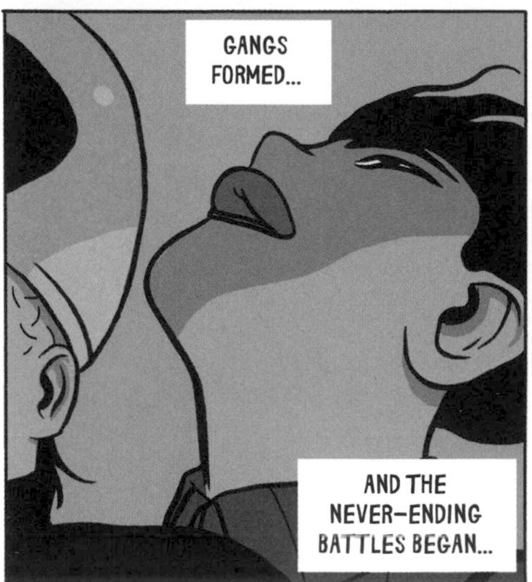
GANGS FORMED...
AND THE NEVER-ENDING BATTLES BEGAN...

BBRRRRRRKKKK
TEACH YOU TO SELL ME PARSLEY!

MOOOOVE!!

BUMP!

....AAAA

AAAA

HEY,
LOSER...

FOR YOUR INFORMATION, IT WASN'T PARSLEY...

IT WAS CORIANDER!!

SCREEECHHH
HA HA
HA HA

WANNA GO SEE RAGS?
I'M GOING TO SEE A LAY-DEE.
YOU'RE DITCHING ME FOR A GIRL?

PUT THIS SOMEWHERE SAFE...
AND YEAH...

RIO
I'M DITCHING YOU FOR A GIRL.

VESS
MY NAME IS CONRAD VESS. AND I NEED YOUR HELP.
A MONTH AGO, MY DAUGHTER WENT MISSING.
THE POLICE HAVE NO LEADS ON HER AT ALL...
AND AS I'M SURE YOU UNDERSTAND, HER MOTHER AND I ARE EXTREMELY WORRIED.
I KNOW SHE WAS FRIENDLY WITH MEMBERS OF YOUR GANGS...
SO I'M OFFERING ONE MILLION POUNDS TO WHOEVER CAN RETURN HER TO ME.
YOU MIGHT KNOW HER...
...AS LOLLY.
WE WOULD HAVE FOUND HER, MR VESS. JUST A LITTLE MORE TIME...
YOU KNOW, CONFIDENCE, WHEN I WORK ON THESE BUILDINGS I'M ALWAYS LET DOWN BY SOMEONE...
WHEN I BUILT EASTFIELDS IT WAS A SUPPLIER AND THEN AN ARCHITECT...
I RARELY GIVE A SECOND CHANCE.
WE'LL FIND HER AGAIN.
I TRULY HOPE SO.
VE

MONDAY

THE GUY WAS A PROPER THUG.

SO I SAID NO I'M NOT A STAR.

STARS SHINE IN THE NIGHT SKY BUT ME, I'M AS DULL AS DIRT...

SELF-DEPRECATION FRAZZLED HIS BRAIN AND HE JUST WALKED OFF SAYING I WAS A FREAK.

BOY, YOU SHOWED YOURSELF UP.

BZT BZT

BZT BZT

NOTHING MUCH. WANNA HOOK UP LATER?

CAN'T, ROSH. MADE PLANS.

WELL, DO YOU WANNA GO SEE TRIANGULAR AT THE CINEMA?

I'VE SEEN IT ALREADY.

SORRY, BRO...

WEDNESDAY

<Messages Kay Contact

Jimmy iz out! Wanna come game?

Message Send

<Messages Kay Contact

Soz. Bizzy. Laterzzz. K

Ok. Later.

Message Send

<Messages Kay Contact

Tomorrow?

Message Send

THURSDAY

ਰੋਸ਼ਨ ਤੂੰ ਇਸ ਹਫਤ ਕੀ ਕਰਨਾ ਹੈ?

ROSHAN, WHAT ARE YOU DOING THIS WEEK?

VESS

FIRST THINGS FIRST... A HAIRCUT.

THEN I NEED TO GET A NEW SHIRT AND COMICS...

THEN NEXT WEEK I HAVE A MEETING WITH THE HEADMASTER.

COUGH LEGO HEAD.

I'M NOT ON YOUR BACK.

ਮੈ ਜਾਣਨਾ ਚਾਹੁੰਦਾ ਹਾ ਕਿ ਤੁਹੀ ਕੀ ਯੋਜਨ ਹੋ?

I WANT TO KNOW WHAT YOU PLAN TO DO NOW?

MAYBE YOU WANT TO GET A JOB AT THE SUPERMARKET?

...OR A SHOP, OR A BUILDING SITE.

YEAH, ROSHAN.

KAY Calling...

YEAH. ROSH IS THAT YOU?

WHERE ARE YOU, MAN?

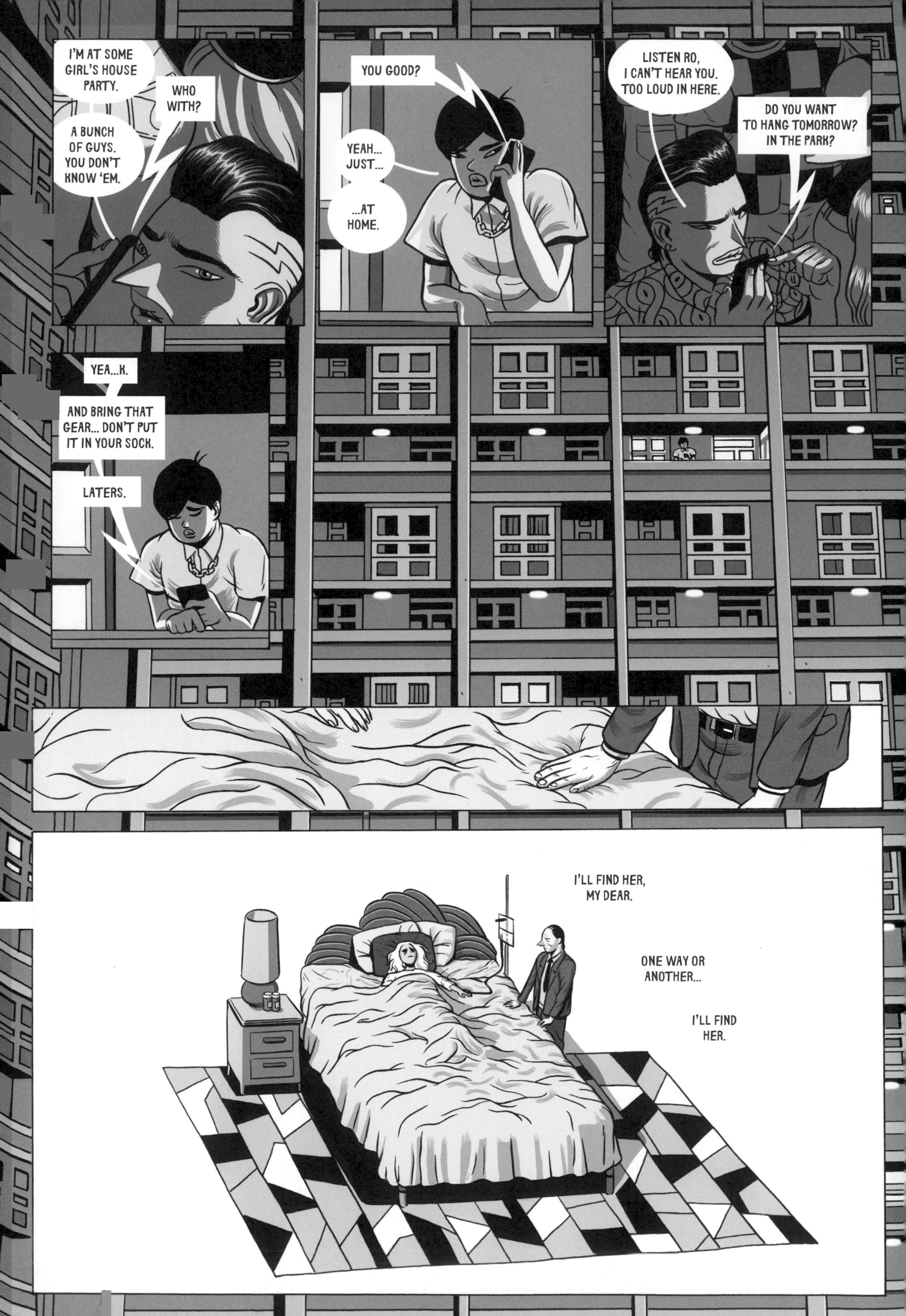
I'M AT SOME GIRL'S HOUSE PARTY.
WHO WITH?
A BUNCH OF GUYS. YOU DON'T KNOW 'EM.
YOU GOOD?
YEAH... JUST...
...AT HOME.
LISTEN RO, I CAN'T HEAR YOU. TOO LOUD IN HERE.
DO YOU WANT TO HANG TOMORROW? IN THE PARK?
YEA...K.
AND BRING THAT GEAR... DON'T PUT IT IN YOUR SOCK.
LATERS.
I'LL FIND HER, MY DEAR.
ONE WAY OR ANOTHER...
I'LL FIND HER.

SATURDAY
OR...
WE COULD GO OVER TO TVC?
I WANNA SEE THAT NEW PROGENITOR DX FIGURE.
IT LOOKS AWESOME!
THERE'S A NEW DESIGN JUST LIKE THE ONE I USED TO HAVE...
TRIPLE LOCK ARMS!
MULTI-COLOUR OPTIONS!
INTER-CHANGEABLE PARTS!
REALLY NOT BOTHERED, ROSH.
BUT...
LET'S GO OVER TO THE MARKET.
I SAID I'D MEET SOMEONE DOWN THERE.
BUT I THOUGHT...
...
THAT'S HER...
OVER THERE.
DOESN'T MATTER...

ROSHAN, THIS...
IS A MONKEY FROM THE ZOO.
AH... THE ELUSIVE ROSHAN.
HI.

I'M LOLLY.

ME?
ELUSIVE?
I'M THE ONE WHO'S BEEN BELLING KAY EVERY DAY.

YEAH... THAT'S MY FAULT.
WE'VE BEEN...
...HANGING OUT...

...A LOT.

SO I FANCY GOING IN TO TOWN. I CAN GET SOME COMICS AND YOU TWO CAN—
I THOUGHT WE'D GET SOME FOOD HERE THEN HANG OUT IN THE PARK...
O...K... LOOK...
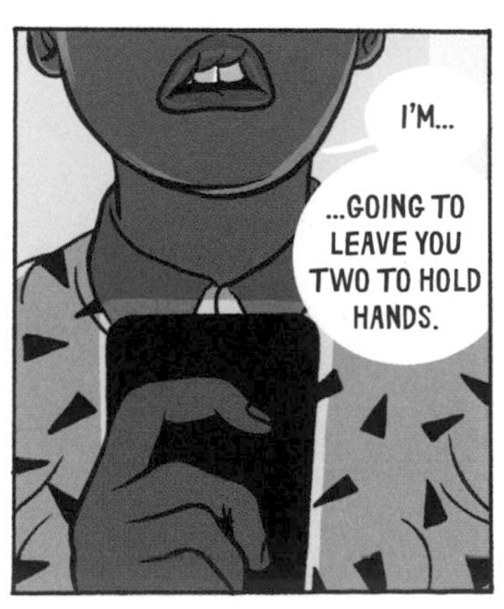
I'M...
...GOING TO LEAVE YOU TWO TO HOLD HANDS.

WHAT?
ROSH, DON'T BE SILLY...

ME?
I HAVEN'T SEEN YOU FOR AGES AND YOU PULL THIS?
PULL WHAT?

LOLLY, I'M SURE YOU'RE NICE AND ALL BUT...
I HAVEN'T SEEN KAY FOR AGES. I THOUGHT WE WERE GOING TO HANG OUT.
LIKE WE USED TO.

WELL MAYBE I SHOULD GO...
...AND YOU TWO CAN BE BUM CHUMS.
LIKE YOU USED TO.

NO NEED TO BE SALTY.
THIS ISN'T SALTY.

I CAN SHOW YOU SALTY IF YOU WANT?
COME ON, YOU TWO...
WHAT ARE YOU DOING?

AZIM'S B
BERBE

IT'S HER. SHE...
IT'S NOT ME KAY DOESN'T WANT TO HANG OUT WITH, STUPID!
LOLLY...

I'M OUT OF HERE, KAY.
THIS BOY IS AN ASS.

BETTER AN ASS THAN A FAT ASS.
SHUT UP, MAN.

WHAT?
SHE CALLED ME A...
GO PLAY WITH YOUR TOYS, ROSHAN.

BETTER THAN PLAYING WITH YOU...
HA HA HA
hehehe
I DON'T MEAN IN A SEXUAL WAY!
PLATONIC...
Hope u n lolly r
Send
Hope u n lolly r v happy tog…
Send
DELETE, DELETE, DELETE...
Send
HEY, BRAH.
HOLIST
ARE YOU KAY?
UH, NO.
SO YOU'RE ROSHAN, RIGHT?
WHERE KAY AT, BRO?

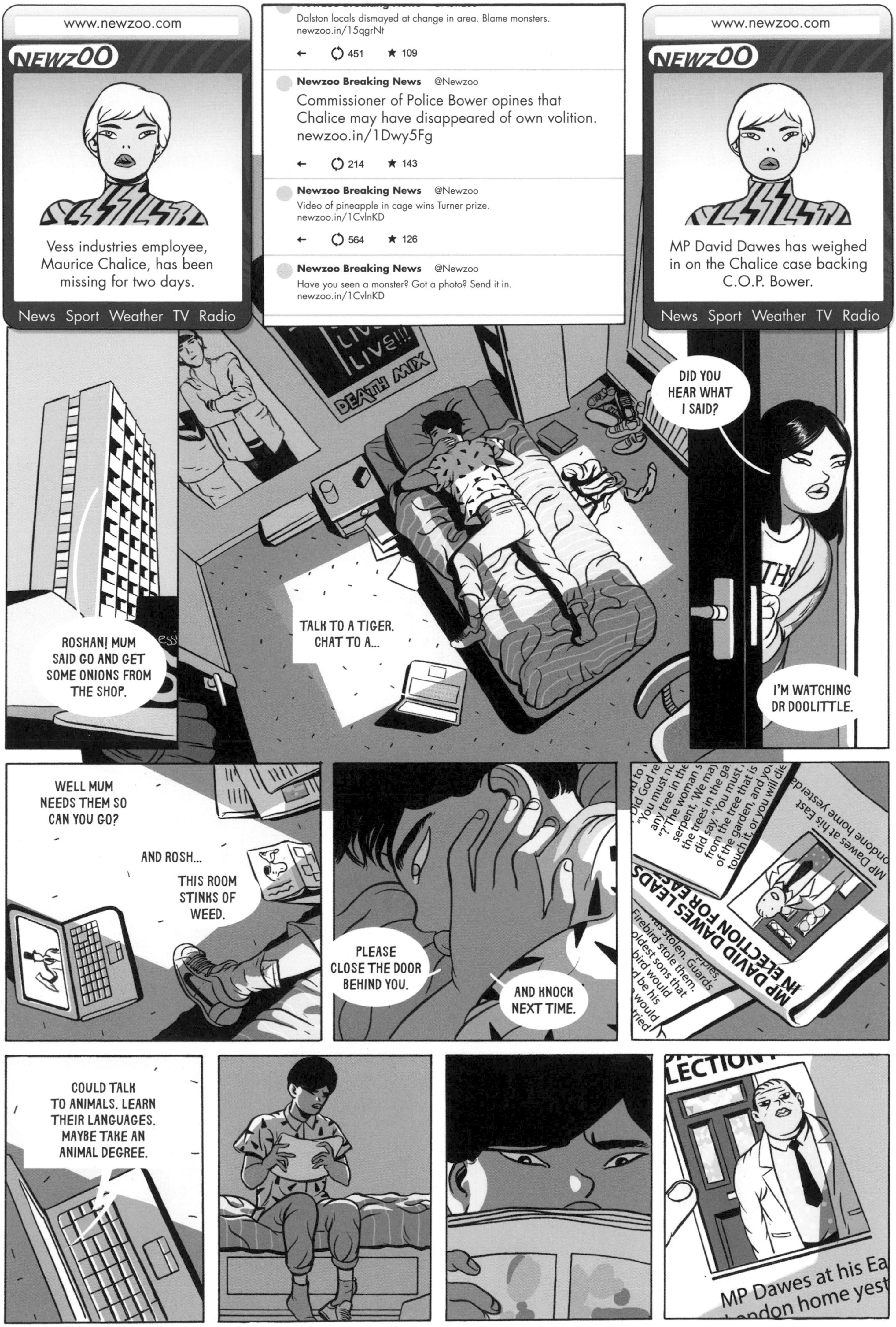

www.newzoo.com

NEWZOO

Vess industries employee, Maurice Chalice, has been missing for two days.

News Sport Weather TV Radio

Dalston locals dismayed at change in area. Blame monsters.
newzoo.in/15qgrNt

451 109

Newzoo Breaking News @Newzoo

Commissioner of Police Bower opines that Chalice may have disappeared of own volition.
newzoo.in/1Dwy5Fg

214 143

Newzoo Breaking News @Newzoo

Video of pineapple in cage wins Turner prize.
newzoo.in/1CvlnKD

564 126

Newzoo Breaking News @Newzoo

Have you seen a monster? Got a photo? Send it in.
newzoo.in/1CvlnKD

www.newzoo.com

NEWZOO

MP David Dawes has weighed in on the Chalice case backing C.O.P. Bower.

News Sport Weather TV Radio

DEATH MIX

ROSHAN! MUM SAID GO AND GET SOME ONIONS FROM THE SHOP.

TALK TO A TIGER. CHAT TO A...

DID YOU HEAR WHAT I SAID?

I'M WATCHING DR DOOLITTLE.

WELL MUM NEEDS THEM SO CAN YOU GO?

AND ROSH...

THIS ROOM STINKS OF WEED.

PLEASE CLOSE THE DOOR BEHIND YOU.

AND KNOCK NEXT TIME.

MP DAVID DAWES LEADS IN ELECTION FOR EAS

crumple

tap tap

gasp

L...
LOLLY?

KAY'S IN TROUBLE!

THEY CAME OUT OF NOWHERE
AND TOOK HIM.

YOU'RE SITTING ON A MONSTER...

SAID THEY WERE TAKING HIM TO THE ZAG.
THE ZAG?
WHAT'S THAT?

NO ONE GETS OUT OF THE ZAG.
RREEET...

RRR...

THEY'RE COMING.
I KNEW THIS WAS THEIR POST CODE BUT...

WHO?
WHO'S COMING?
THE HARD FACES.
I'VE GOT TO GET OUT OF HERE.
DO YOU WANT TO HELP?
I...
I'M NOT...
ROSHAN!
MUM'S COMING WITH HER SHOE!
THUDDD

WE'VE BEEN LOOKING FOR YOU ALL OVER DALSTON.
ROOFTOPS, PARKS, ALLEYWAYS, GUTTERS...
AND HERE YOU ARE...
...RUNNING TO YOUR BOYFRIEND FOR HELP.
LIKE A LITTLE GIRL.

I'M NOT HER BOY—
SO UNLESS HE'S SOME SORT OF...

...SECRET WEAPON...

...YOU'D BEST GET DOWN OFF YOUR PET AND COME WITH US.
I'M TOO HOT TO WAIT FOR LONG.

CLIP CLOP

NEANA TAKE A REST.
I KNOW YOU HARD FACES THINK YOU'RE BAD BUT...

NOT ONE OF YOU ARE AS HARD AS ME.

I'M A BAD BITCH.

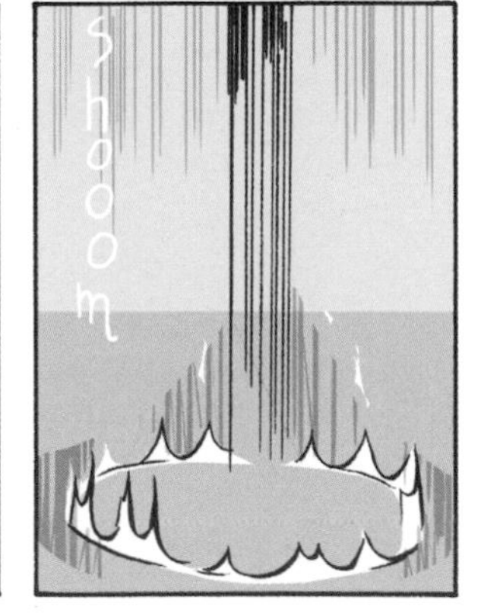
shooom

WHERE THE HELL...?

WHERE IS SHE?
I CAN'T SEE A...
WHA.?!
SHOOM
SHOOT HER!
OW!
THUDDDD
MY BOOBS...
FOOM
FOOM
FOOM
fst.
GUNNK!

WOW.

UUH...

LET'S GET OUT OF HERE, NEANA.

IT'S TIME FOR SOME EXPOSITION.

www.newzoo.com

NEWZOO

A fifth businessman goes missing. Report follows our special on robot dogs: urban policing for the future?

News Sport Weather TV Radio

LET ME GO AND WE'LL FORGET THIS EVER HAPPENED.

NO HARD FEELINGS.

THERE ARE TWELVE OTHER GANGS OUT THERE LOOKING FOR LOLLY.

AND THEY'LL BE SEARCHING ALL OVER.

TRYING TO FIGURE OUT WHERE SHE MIGHT BE.

I DON'T KNOW WHERE THE ZAG IS.
I NEVER ACTUALLY WENT THERE...
I KNOW THE GUYS THAT TOOK KAY...
WHAT?
THE TEENAGE MUTANT DALSTON BASTARDS.
WE HUNG OUT FOR A FEW MONTHS.
THEY WERE DOING SOMETHING OVER THERE AT THE ZAG.
SOMETHING REALLY MESSED UP.
I DIDN'T WANT TO GET INVOLVED SO...
I SPLIT.
IT'S BECAUSE OF YOU?
THEY'VE TAKEN KAY BECAUSE OF YOU?
I DON'T...
...I'M NOT SURE.
ALRIGHT, NEANA...
TAKE IT EASY, LOVE.

I'VE BEEN WRACKING MY BRAINS TRYING TO WORK OUT WHY THEY'RE ALL AFTER ME.
WHAT I'VE DONE.

WHO'S AFTER YOU?
GANG KIDS.
FOR THE LAST WEEK THEY'VE BEEN FOLLOWING ME OR HASSLING ME.
ASKING TO MEET WHEN I BARELY KNOW THEM.

THIS JUST GETS BETTER AND BETTER.

NEANA SHOULD BE FINE NOW.
JUST NEEDS TO REST FOR A LITTLE WHILE.

WE'RE CONNECTED, YOU SEE.
LIKE A SAND TIMER.
REEEETT:

WHEN SHE RESTS, I GET AN INCREDIBLE STRENGTH...
...AND VICE VERSA.

I DIDN'T THINK IT WAS 'COS YOU'D HAD A BIG BREAKFAST.
DID KAY KNOW ABOUT ALL THIS?
UH... NO.

WE MET WHEN HE WAS RIDING HIS SCOOTER IN THE PARK, LIKE A MORON. SO I CALLED HIM OUT.
YOU SHOULD GET ON THE BACK.
THERE'S ROOM FOR TWO MORONS ON HERE.

I WAS SLEEPING ON MY FRIEND'S FLOOR AFTER MY PARENTS KICKED ME OUT.
I NEEDED SOME FUN.

AND I NEVER FOUND THE RIGHT TIME TO TELL HIM.

SO LET ME GET THIS STRAIGHT.
YOUR OLD GANG KIDNAPPED KAY.
WE NEED TO GET TO THIS ZAG PLACE BUT YOU DON'T KNOW WHERE IT IS.
AND ALL THE GANGS IN DALSTON ARE AFTER YOU?
OH AND I NEED TO ASK...

WHAT IS A BAD BITCH AND HOW DO I BECOME ONE?

LOOK, IF YOU WANT TO GO, I GET IT...
NO WAY. I THINK KAY NEEDS ME TO LOOK OUT FOR HIM.

SO HOW DO WE FIND THIS BLOODY ZAG?
THERE'S A LADY...
...A FORTUNE TELLER.
SHE'S A LADY WHO SEES THINGS, KNOWS THINGS.

HER NAME IS AFSA AL ANSARI.
EASY PEASY.
IT'S UNDER EASTFIELD.
THE SHOPPING CENTRE.
LAST TIME I SAW YOU I PREDICTED YOU'D MEET A NEW BOY...

IS THIS HE?
NO NO NO.
THIS IS ANOTHER GUY.
YOU HAVE TWO?
HE'S NOT ANOTHER GUY
HE'S THE OTHER ONE'S FRIEND.
YOU'RE SEEING TWO FRIENDS?
RISKY.

NO. I...
UH...
COULD I USE YOUR BATHROOM?
YES. FOLLOW ME.

BUT THEN WE REALLY SHOULD BE GOING.

YOU'LL STAY FOR TEA FIRST.
AISHA, BE POLITE TO THE BOY.

SHOW ME YOUR HAND.

QUICK, BEFORE SHE COMES BACK.
MY BIBI CAN'T SEE FURTHER THAN HER NOSE.

I CAN SEE THE FUTURE.

BUT I DON'T WANT TO KNOW MY FUTURE.
SHHH.
WHO WOULDN'T WANT TO KNOW WHAT'S TO COME?

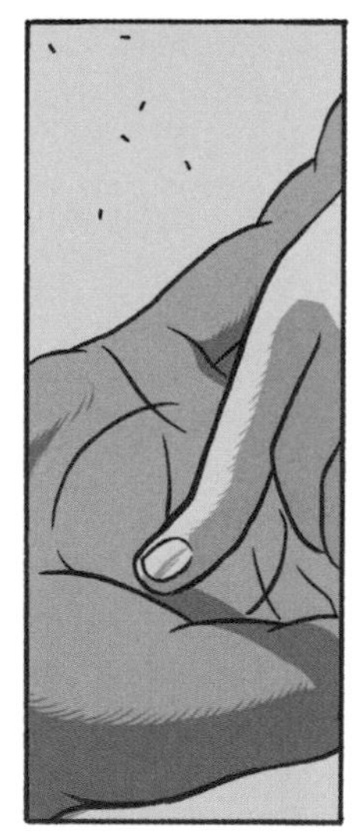

I... SEE...
A DARK BEHEMOTH.
FACE TO FACE...
WITH SOMEONE.
WITH YOU!

THE MONSTER WILL KILL YOU.
IT WILL KILL YOUR FRIENDS.
THERE IS NO WAY TO STOP IT.
NO WAY...
UNLESS...

FALADA...

SHE'S COMING BACK.

GOOGLE FALADA.

BUT
WHAT...?
DO AS I SAY.
IT WILL SAVE YOU TONIGHT.

HERE WE ARE.
NICE CUP OF TEA.
I HOPE AISHA HASN'T BEEN ANNOYING YOU.
NO.

NOT AT ALL.

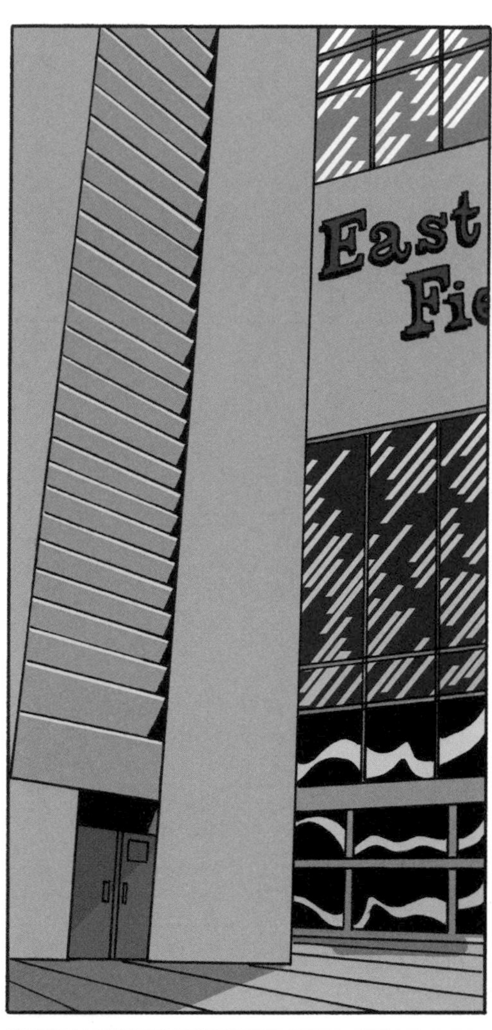
East
Fie

EXIT
BANG!
DNG!

BANG!

BANG!
-3
DNG!

DNG!
-5

-91
BANG!

BANG!

BANG!
DNG!
THEY WON'T LISTEN.
THEY WON'T EVEN TELL US WHY WE'RE HERE.

I'VE BEEN IN HERE FOR FOUR DAYS.
SLEEPING ON THE FLOOR. EATING THEIR SLOP.
HELP

THAT GUY WAS HERE WHEN I GOT HERE.
CIRCLE... A CIRCLE...

FROM THE LITTLE HE'S SAID, I THINK HE WENT INTO THAT... MAZE...
WITH A NUMBER OF OTHERS...

BUT HE WAS THE ONLY ONE TO ESCAPE.
CIRCLE IN MY POCKET.
KEEP IT IN MY POCKET...

A MAZE?

I DON'T KNOW MUCH MORE.
I JUST NEED TO TELL MY WIFE THAT I'M ALRIGHT.
THAT I'LL BE HOME SOON.

SHE'LL BE SO WORRIED.

WHY ARE YOU IN HERE?

CONRAD VESS IS WHY.
WE WERE FRIENDS. PARTNERS.
VESS LTD. WENT GLOBAL UNDER OUR MANAGEMENT.
I SACRIFICED EVERYTHING.

BARELY SAW MY FAMILY...

WHO ARE YOU?

I'M MAURICE CHALICE.

THE HAWK AND THE NI
I'M FINE WITH HEIGHTS.

OPEN SPACES...
BUT ENCLOSED PLACES LIKE THE UNDERGROUND...
WHATEVS.
COME LOOK AT THIS.

WE'RE GOING THROUGH THESE AREAS TO GET TO EASTFIELD. AND WE'RE GOING TO HAVE TO GET PAST THESE GANGS TO GET THERE.
KOS.
HE'S OLDER THAN THE REST OF US AND HAS AN ARMY OF MONSTERS. LITERALLY A WHOLE ARMY.
THE SUPPER HORSES.
THESE GUYS ARE MEAN. THEIR MOTTO IS 'YOU'RE WITH US OR YOU'RE IN HELL'. THEY LIKE TO FIGHT. RUMOUR HAS IT THAT THEIR LEADER IS THE SON OF A PROMINENT POLITICIAN.
TEKTON SMART BOYS.
THEY BELIEVE THAT THEY ARE THE CHOSEN FUTURE.
WICK DEEP THOUGHT.
THEIR LEADER FOUGHT A WHOLE OTHER GANG AND WON. NO ONE KNOWS HOW BUT EVERYONE IS SCARED OF THE DUDE NOW.
keep a place for me... I'll
CLISSOLD PARK
BALLS POND
KINGSLAND ROAD
QUEENSBRIDGE
H.P.
HACKNEY
THIS IS OUR BUS.
I THINK WE'D BETTER GO UPSTAIRS...
...THAT GUY REEKS.
GO SIT NEXT TO HIM.

STEEZ LADIES.
THE ONLY GANG I'D JOIN BUT I WOULDN'T WANT TO MESS WITH.
RED EYES.
THEY'RE LIKE A FAMILY AND THEY ALL HAVE THE SAME KIND OF MONSTER — THE EYES.
TIN SISTERS.
THEY RULE THEIR PATCH HARD. THEIR MONSTERS OPERATE TOGETHER AND ALMOST SEEM TO BE PSYCHIC.
THE CRYING FIVES.
THEIR LIST OF CRIMES IS LONG. BURNING SHOPS, ROBBING, MUGGING... IT GOES ON AND ON.
HOMERTON HIGH
CASSLAND
VICKY PARK
H WICK
Endhiran.
Runa- 0795 263 25
MONSTERS WON'T GET A SNIFF OF ME IF THEY CATCH A WHIFF OF HIM.
REALLY?
DO WE REALLY HAVE TO SIT HERE?
UNTIL YOU APOLOGISE.

APOLOGISE?
SAID ANYTHING YOU REGRET, ROSHAN?
I DON'T KNOW WHAT YOU'RE TALKING ABOUT.

WE ALL SAY THINGS WE DON'T MEAN, DON'T WE?
THINGS THAT MIGHT BE... TROUBLESOME.
DON'T WE?
I'M GOING TO BE SICK.

WHAT?
FAT ASS?
OH... THAT.
LOOK, I DIDN'T MEAN...
YOU CALLED ME AN ASS...

YOU ARE AN ASS.

SO THAT GIRL, AISHA...
SHE READ YOUR PALM, RIGHT?

YEAH, SO?
YOUR FUTURE HAS SOMETHING CRAZY COMING UP...
YOU'RE SPECIAL, RIGHT?

YOU DIDN'T BELIEVE HER, DID YOU?
HA HA
AISHA DOES THAT TO EVERYONE.
LADIES AND GENTLEMEN...

DUE TO TECHNICAL ISSUES THIS VEHICLE...
WILL BE TERMINATING AT THE NEXT STOP.
GREAT.
WORLD'S SLOWEST RESCUE MISSION EVER.

I HAVE GOOD NEWS, FRANCES.

AFTER ALL THIS TIME TRYING TO FIND HER, SHE'S MAKING HER WAY TO US.
WE WON'T NEED TO WORRY ANYMORE.
SHE'S COMING HOME.

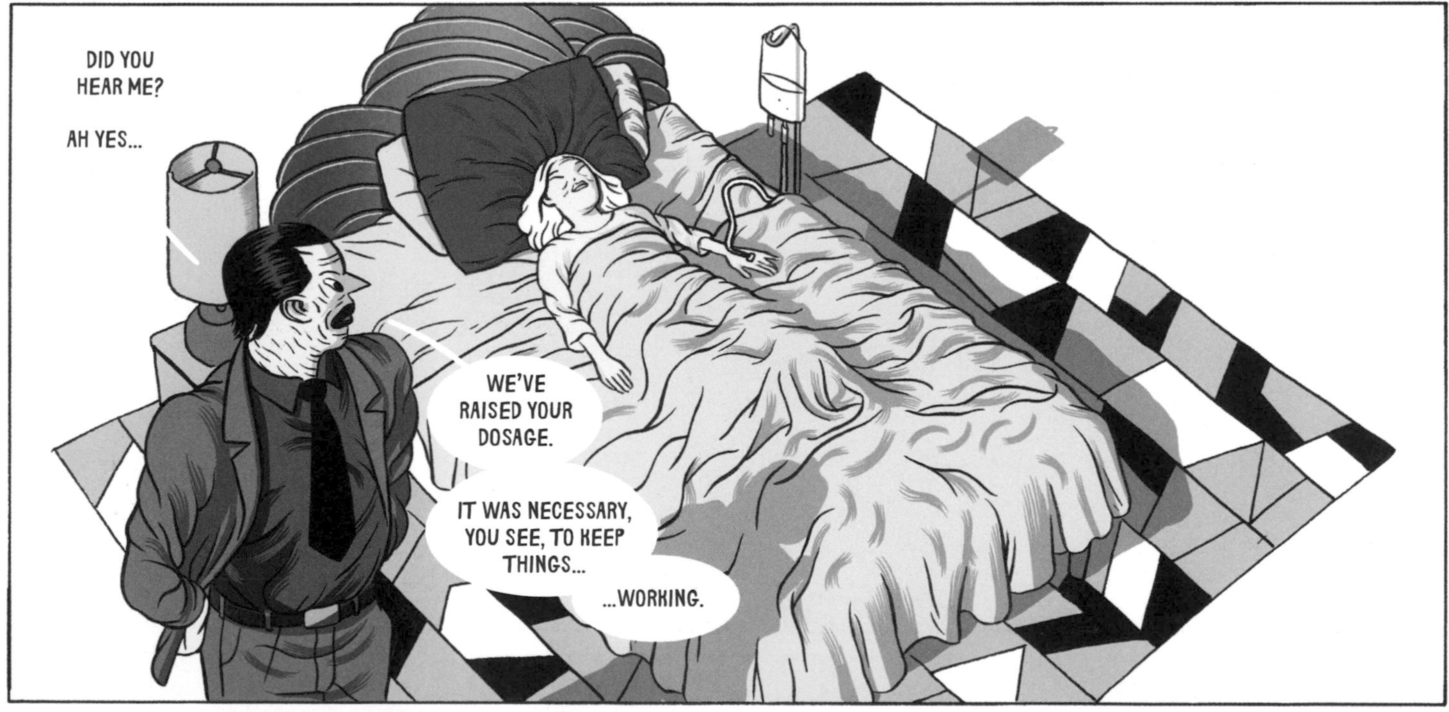
DID YOU HEAR ME?
AH YES...
WE'VE RAISED YOUR DOSAGE.
IT WAS NECESSARY, YOU SEE, TO KEEP THINGS...
...WORKING.

LOLLY WILL BE BACK SOON. THEN WE CAN ALL MOVE ON.

AND LET'S GET RID OF THAT SCULPTURE.
I'VE ALWAYS HATED IT.

SNIFF
SNIFF
IS IT HER?
TITO, MERRICK! CALL THE OTHERS.
LET'S GO!
BDOM
BDOM
BBBBBB
rustle
rustle

IT WAS DURING THE RIOTS...

I WENT INTO A SUPERMARKET THAT HAD BEEN LOOTED.

I JUST WANTED TO SEE HOW BAD IT WAS FOR MYSELF.

THERE WAS NOTHING LEFT IN THERE.

RANSACKED.

I PICKED UP A BOTTLE OF WATER, JUST...

I DON'T KNOW WHY.

STEPPED OUT OF THE SHOP AND THE FIVE-O WERE WAITING.

NIHILISM OF AN ILLITERATE YOUTH, HE SAID.

SOCIETY GONE TO THE DOGS.

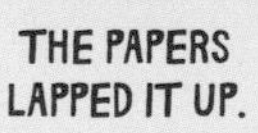

SO WHEN I WAS SENTENCED...

Rule of the

London riots: Superbuy water thief jailed for six months

A school student with no criminal record wa Thursday for stealing a £1.50 case of bottled

MAN, MY PARENTS HATED ME.

VESS
HOMES
BDOM
BDOM
BBBBBB
I THINK PARENTS ARE SUPPOSED TO HATE THEIR KIDS.
MY MUM HATES ME.

IT IS HER, RIGHT?

THE FEELING'S MUTUAL REALLY.

SPNG

BDOM
BDOM
BBBBBB

I'M SURE IT'S NOT.
THERE'S A REASON I HAD TO LEAVE HOME, YOU KNOW.

BDOM
BDOM
BKISH!
WHA?
FSHHHH
NEANA!
HOW ARE YOU, BABY?
UH... LOLLY. LOOK ON THE ROOF.
BDOM
BDOM
BBBBBB
GO!

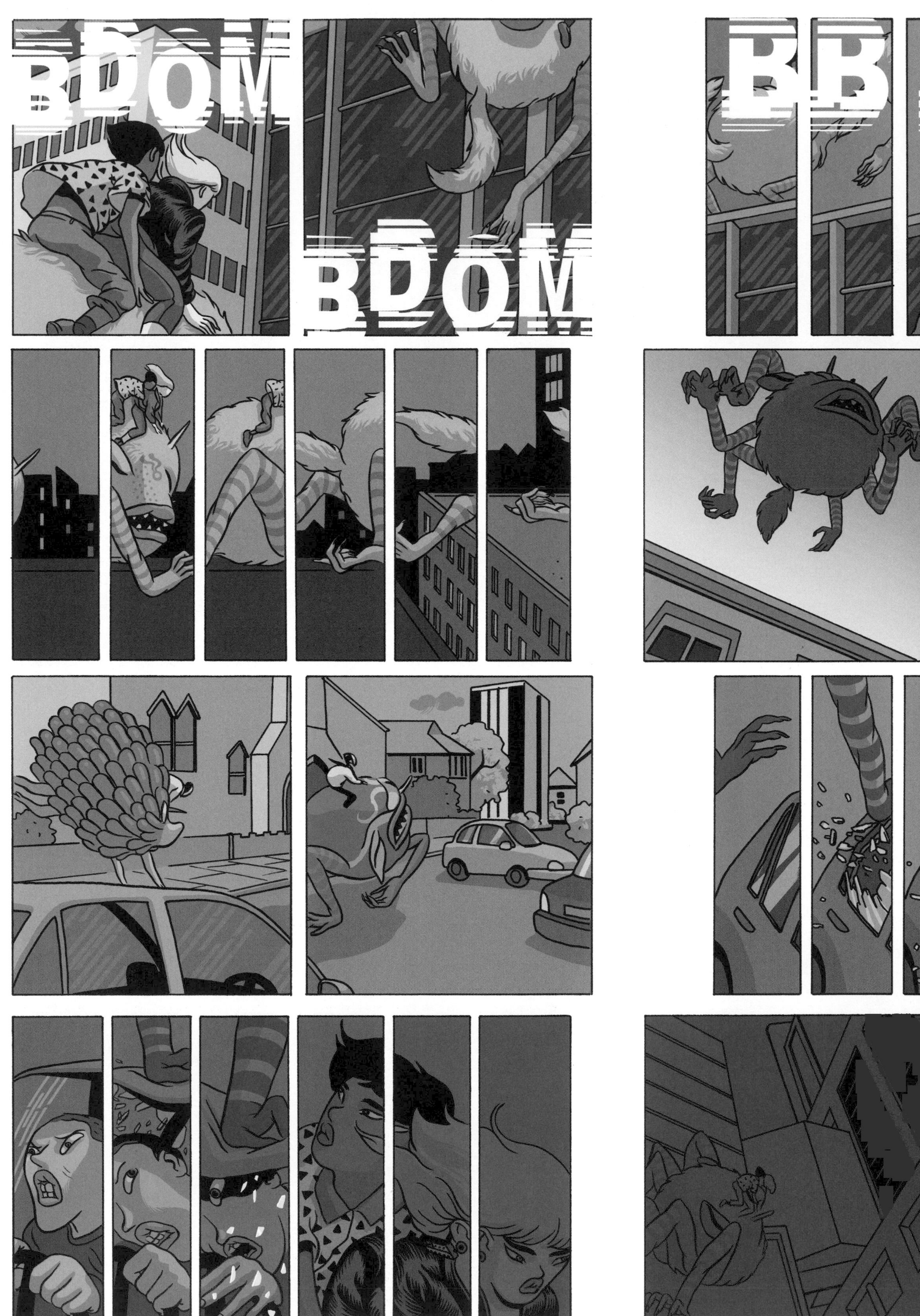
BDOM
BDOM

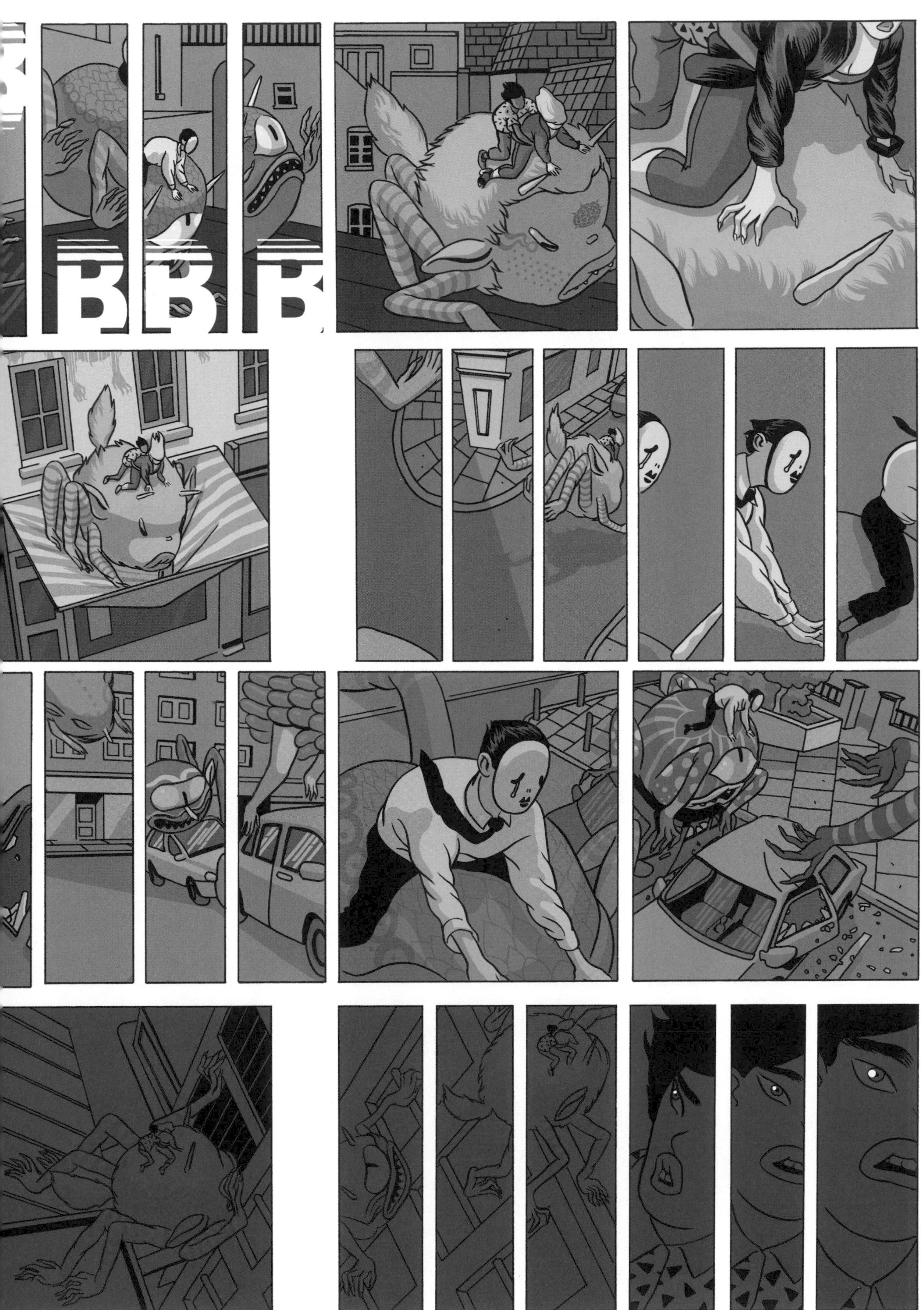

AAAAAAAA

LOLLY!
WE JUST WANT TO TALK!

THE WALL...

I'VE GOT AN IDEA.

I TOLD YOU THIS WAS THE WRONG WAY.

THIS ISN'T THE WRONG WAY. I JUST... AAHHH!

EEEEEEEEEE

YOUR BOYFRIEND ISN'T LONG FOR THIS WORLD.

HE GOES INTO THE ZAG...
TONIGHT.

NOT YET. NOT YET.

WE CAN TAKE YOU TO HIM IF YOU LIKE.

NOW!

YOU'LL NEVER MAKE IT IN TIME!

YOUR BOY'S DEAD, LOLLY!
DEAD!

THAT WAS ROUGH...
I THINK THERE'S MORE TO COME.

ARE WE JUST GOING TO SIT HERE AND WAIT UNTIL THEY PUT US IN THE MAZE?
THERE MUST BE SOME WAY OUT.
IF I GET OUT OF HERE...
I'M GOING TO HOLD MY SON SO TIGHT.

Ga

IF WE GO BACK WE COULD GET THE OVERGROUND STRAIGHT TO STRATFORD?

THAT WAY WE CAN AVOID THE...
ROSHAN?

WHAT IS IT?

I DIDN'T THINK IT WOULD BE THIS CRAZY.
AND I DON'T WANT TO GET IN TROUBLE WITH THE LAW AGAIN...

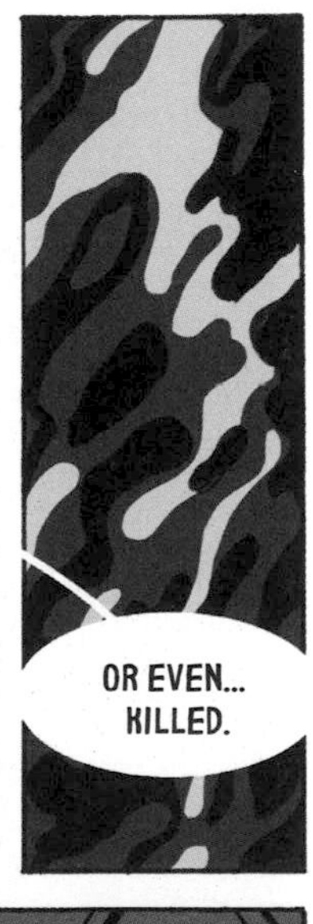
OR EVEN... KILLED.

YOU WANT TO QUIT?
IF KAY CAN'T RELY ON YOU NOW, WHEN HE REALLY NEEDS YOU THEN YOU'RE NOT MUCH OF A FRIEND, ARE YOU?
SO GO...

..AND I'M BETTER OFF WITHOUT YOU.
LOLLY.. THIS IS YOUR WORLD, NOT MINE.

YEAH...
WELL MAYBE IT'S TIME YOU WENT BACK HOME TO MUMMY...

... AND I'LL FIND KAY IN THIS CRAZY WORLD.

SIR, COMMISSIONER BOWER HAS INFORMED US THAT HE IS ON HIS WAY TO EASTFIELD.
DAWES, HOWEVER, WILL NOT BE ATTENDING TONIGHT.

READY THE CAR.

RRRRUMBLE

UH-OH.

Falada
Soosle Search
Falada
Falada horse
Falada leisure
Falada sport
Falada meaning
Enna burning

he Goose Girl
Interpedia, the free encyclo
For other uses, see The Go

Synopsis [edit]
A widowed queen sends her daughter to her bridegroom in a faraway land. She sends her with a waiting maid. The princess's horse is named Falada, and he is magical for he can speak. The princess is given a special charm by her

SCROLL
SCROLL
MAYBE LOLLY WAS RIGHT

Exit

MAYBE THAT GIRL AISHA WAS TALKING CRAP.

BBBBZZZ

I CAN SEE YOU'RE IN.
THE LIGHTS ARE ON.

I GOT SIX MONTHS BECAUSE OF YOU
SIX MONTHS FOR A BOTTLE OF WATER.

JEREMY BLUNT STOLE FIFTY THOUSAND POUNDS...
... AND DIDN'T SERVE A SINGLE DAY.

HE'S A POLITICIAN LIKE YOU.

IS THAT FAIR, MR DAWES?

WELCOME, FRIENDS. TONIGHT'S GAME IS STARTING AT TEN THOUSAND.
PLEASE PLACE YOUR BETS.
I'M SURE TONIGHT'S CONTESTANTS WILL HAVE YOUR FULL APPROVAL.
WE ALL HAVE BAD WEEKS NOW AND AGAIN.
I HOPE YOU HAVE SOMETHING BETTER THAN LAST WEEK'S POOR LOT!
YOU KNOW ALL ABOUT BAD WEEKS, DON'T YOU GIDEON?
YOU'RE AMONG FRIENDS NOW. TELL US, HAS NEWZOO BEEN HACKING?
I GIVE PEOPLE WHAT THEY NEED, NOT WHAT THEY WANT.
HA HA HA
GENTLEMEN, HERE ARE YOUR COMPETITORS.
CODENAMED AS EVER.
LAST WEEK'S WINNER,
QUEEQUEG.
HA HA HA HA HA HA HA HA HA HA
OUR FIRST NEW CONTESTANT...
MOBY.
LASTLY, AND I DARE SAY THE FAVOURITE...
AHAB.

ROSHAN?

I DON'T WANT TO FALL OUT.
NOT AGAIN.

THIS IS DAVID DAWES' HOUSE.
AND?
AND I WANT HIM TO COME OUT AND TALK TO ME.
SIGH.

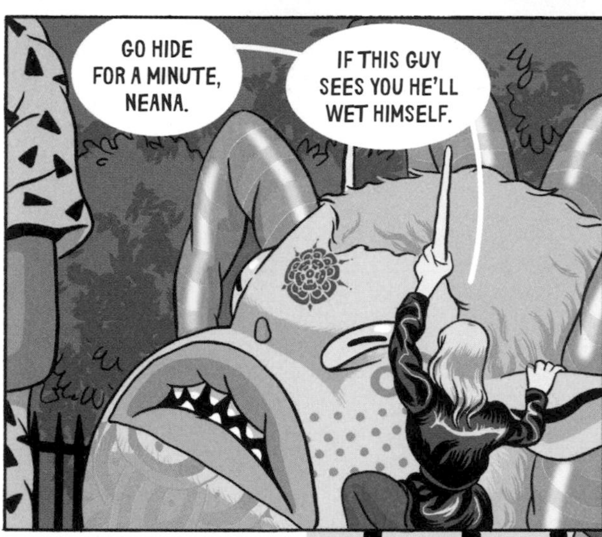
GO HIDE FOR A MINUTE, NEANA.
IF THIS GUY SEES YOU HE'LL WET HIMSELF.

HOW LONG ARE YOU PLANNING ON WAIT..

..ING?

WE NEED TO GO.
NOW.

CLIC CLAK
CLIC CLAK
I SWEAR DAWES SAW ME.

HE WAS ON HIS PHONE BUT HE LOOKED RIGHT AT ME.
JUST GET A MOVE ON, WILL YOU?

I'M MOVING! I'M MOVING!
POLICE

POLICE

HELLO, ROSHAN.
CAN WE HAVE A WORD?

WAIT... WAIT...
huf..
I NEED TO STOP...
huf..
huf..
JUST FOR A MINUTE...
ONE MINUTE...
GOD, I AM SO OUT OF SHAPE... AS SOON AS I'M OUT OF HERE I'M GOING TO THE GYM.
MAURICE... WE REALLY NEED TO KEEP MOVING.
huf..
huf..
I'M COMING...
B...
B...B... B...B...
BEHIND YOU!

AAAARRRHH!!
MY EYE!
GET OFF HIM!
SSSSSS!
GRRRRRRR
MOVE, SON...
MAURICE?
GET OUT OF HERE!
RUN!
AAAAAARGHH!!!
HA HA! YOU LOSE BOWER.
FAT MAN DIDN'T HAVE A CHANCE.

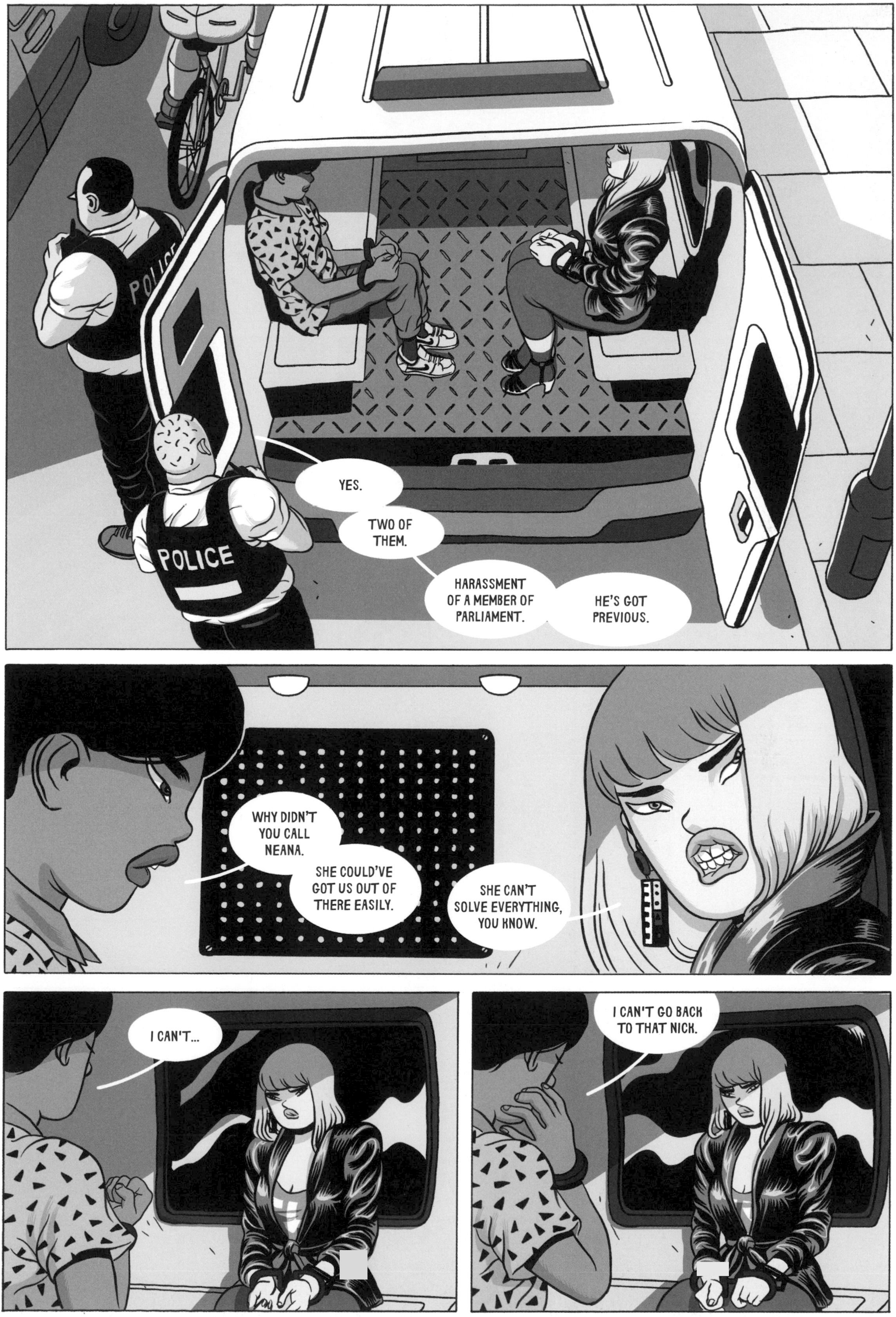

YES.
TWO OF THEM.
HARASSMENT OF A MEMBER OF PARLIAMENT.
HE'S GOT PREVIOUS.

WHAT?

I CAN'T BELIEVE YOU WERE SO FUCKING STUPID.
WHAT DID YOU THINK WAS GOING TO HAPPEN?

THAT DAWES WOULD COME OUT OF HIS HOUSE AND APOLOGISE?
OOOOH ROSHAN. I'M SOOO SORRY THAT I PUT YOU IN THE NEWSPAPERS.

I REALLY SHOULD HAVE CONSIDERED YOUR SOCIO-ECONOMIC BACKGROUND.
AFTER ALL...

IT WAS ONLY...
A BOTTLE...
OF WATER.

POL

YOU THINK I WANTED THIS TO HAPPEN?

I REALLY DON'T KNOW WHAT YOU WANT.
I KNOW WHAT I WANT.
I WANT TO GET KAY OUT OF THAT PLACE.

ALL ABOUT KAY, ISN'T IT?
IT'S ALWAYS ABOUT KAY.
MY MUM LOVES HIM, Y'KNOW.
DAD TOO.
I GO ANYWHERE AND PEOPLE ARE LIKE 'WHERE'S KAY?' 'HOW IS HE?'

THE GIRLS IN MY CLASS.
THE BOYS IN MY CLASS.
MR SULLIVAN, MR CORNER SHOP, MR GREY FLAT TOP.
KAY. KAY. KAY.

GREY FLAT TOP?

AND WEARING RED SPEX?
MAYBE... YEAH I THINK SO...

IT WAS YOU ALL ALONG.

HUH?

HIS NAME IS CONFIDENCE...
...AND HE'S THE LEADER OF TEENAGE MUTANT DALSTON BASTARDS.
YOU TOLD HIM THAT ME AND KAY WERE IN THE PARK, DIDN'T YOU?

I DIDN'T KNOW HE...
I DIDN'T KNOW THIS WOULD HAPPEN.

HOMES
2/3 BEDROOM ST
POLICE

OFFICER COLLING. 15–2 REQUESTING A CHANGE OF DESTINATION.
WHAT?

CONTROL. THIS IS OFFICER COLLING. WHAT IS THE REQUEST?
THIS IS COMMISSIONER BOWER. TAKE THE TWO DETAINED B.O.P.'S TO EASTFIELD CAR PARK D. A REPRESENTATIVE WILL MEET YOU THERE.

COMMISSIONER, THIS IS HIGHLY IRREGULAR...
THIS IS NEITHER THE TIME NOR PLACE TO QUESTION MY ORDERS, COLLING.

BUT SIR, WE'VE CALLED THE KIDS IN AT BETHNAL GREEN STATION.
IT'S A MINOR OFFENCE AND THE DUTY SERGEANT...
I NEED THE TWO OF THEM DELIVERED AS PER MY DETAILS.

DO AS YOU ARE TOLD.
YES, SIR.

SCREEEECH
BEEEEEEP!

NOT YOU, TOO.
I DON'T EVEN KNOW YOUR NAME.
IS THIS...
CHALK?

CONRAD?
WHAT'S GOING ON? WHERE ARE THE POLICE?
YOU KNOW THIS GUY?

HE'S MY STEPFATHER.
WHEN I FIRST MET YOUR MOTHER, SHE WAS MUCH LIKE YOU.
STRONG AND WILFUL.
AND SHE HAD A MONSTER AS YOU DO.

SHE THOUGHT I WAS NAÏVE... GULLIBLE.
IT WAS ONLY WHEN I BECAME WEALTHY AND SHE WAS SINGLE WITH A BABY THAT WE WED.

AND NOW HER MONSTER GROWS WEAK...
AND I NEED A NEW ONE FOR MY MAZE.
A STRONG, YOUNG MONSTER.

YOU CAN'T...
NOT NEANA.
YES, LOLLY. WE FOUND HER OUTSIDE THE SHOPPING CENTRE.

DON'T FRET.
YOU'LL BE HAVING A NICE LONG REST...

LIKE YOUR MOTHER.

THIS LINK YOU HAVE WITH THOSE THINGS...
VERY CONVENIENT.
MR VESS!

WE HAVE EVANS, SIR.
I SHOULD'VE KNOWN YOU'D BE BEHIND THIS, VESS.

YOU MADE ALL THE WRONG CHOICES, EVANS.

PUT HIM IN.
BRING THOSE TWO UP TO THE VIEWING PLATFORM.

YOU WON'T GET AWAY WITH THIS, VESS!
I'LL MAKE SURE OF IT.

HEY, STOP!

WHA?

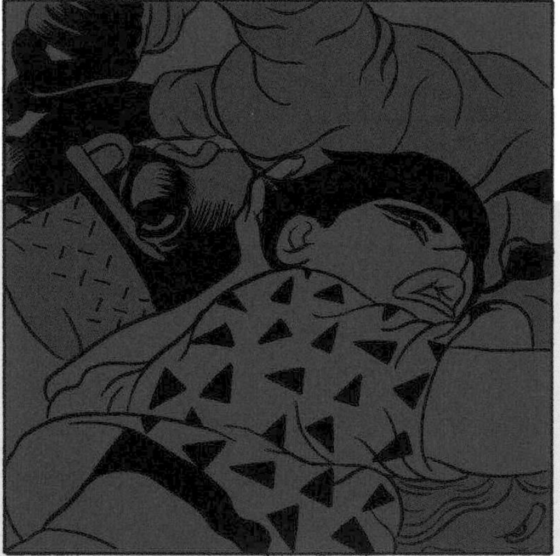

WELL...
THAT'S THE FIRST TIME I'VE SEEN SOMEONE WANT TO GO IN.
ROSHAN!

SHOOOM

LET ME OUT!
SO YOU KNOW THIS PLACE. IS THERE SOME WAY OUT?
GO SCREW YOURSELF, YOU ARSE!
HELPFUL...
OH MAN.
clack
clack
clack
clack
clack
clack
OH CRAP.

ISN'T THAT SWEET. THE TWO OF THEM MEETING LIKE THAT.
I ALWAYS THOUGHT I COULD TRUST YOU, CONRAD.
WHY ARE YOU DOING THIS?
LONDON IS GROWING.
DALSTON IS CHANGING BEFORE OUR EYES.
INVESTORS FROM AROUND THE WORLD ARE BUYING HERE. FROM CHINA, INDIA, AMERICA, SAUDI ARABIA.
BANKERS, POLITICIANS, SPORTSMEN...
AND WHAT DO MOST COMPANIES USE TO ENTICE THEM?
A MEAL? A NIGHT AT THE THEATRE?
THE MEN WHO ARE HERE DON'T CARE ABOUT THOSE THINGS, BUT THIS...
THIS IS ENTERTAINMENT.
IT'S BARBARIC.
WHAT DO I DO? WHAT DO I DO? WHAT DO I DO?
WHAT DO I...
...DO?
BACK!
GET BACK!
I'M IN THE CIRCLE!
I'M IN THE CIRCLE.
SNIFF SNIFF

clack
clack
STILL IN THE CIRCLE...
...YOU STUPID BEAST.
clack
clack
YEAH. GOOD RIDDANCE.
SNIFF
SNIFF
SNIFF
CLEVER BOY.
AND YET YOU PICKED THE OTHER ONE?
ARE YOU SURE YOU'VE MADE THE RIGHT CHOICE?

I CAN'T BELIEVE THAT YOU CAME FOR ME.
I THOUGHT I WAS DONE FOR.
KAY, LOLLY IS HERE TOO. SHE'S IN TROUBLE.
WHAT DO YOU MEAN?
WHERE IS SHE?
IN SOME SORT OF VIEWING ROOM UPSTAIRS WITH HER STEPDAD.
WELL... LET'S GET HER.
NO, YOU'RE GOING TO HER.
I'LL HOLD OFF THIS MONSTER.
WHAT?
I'LL GIVE YOU TIME TO GET AWAY.
TO GET OUT.
I THINK I KNOW HOW.
I THINK.
RO...
I'LL SEE YOU IN A BIT, YEAH?
IF YOU'RE SURE.

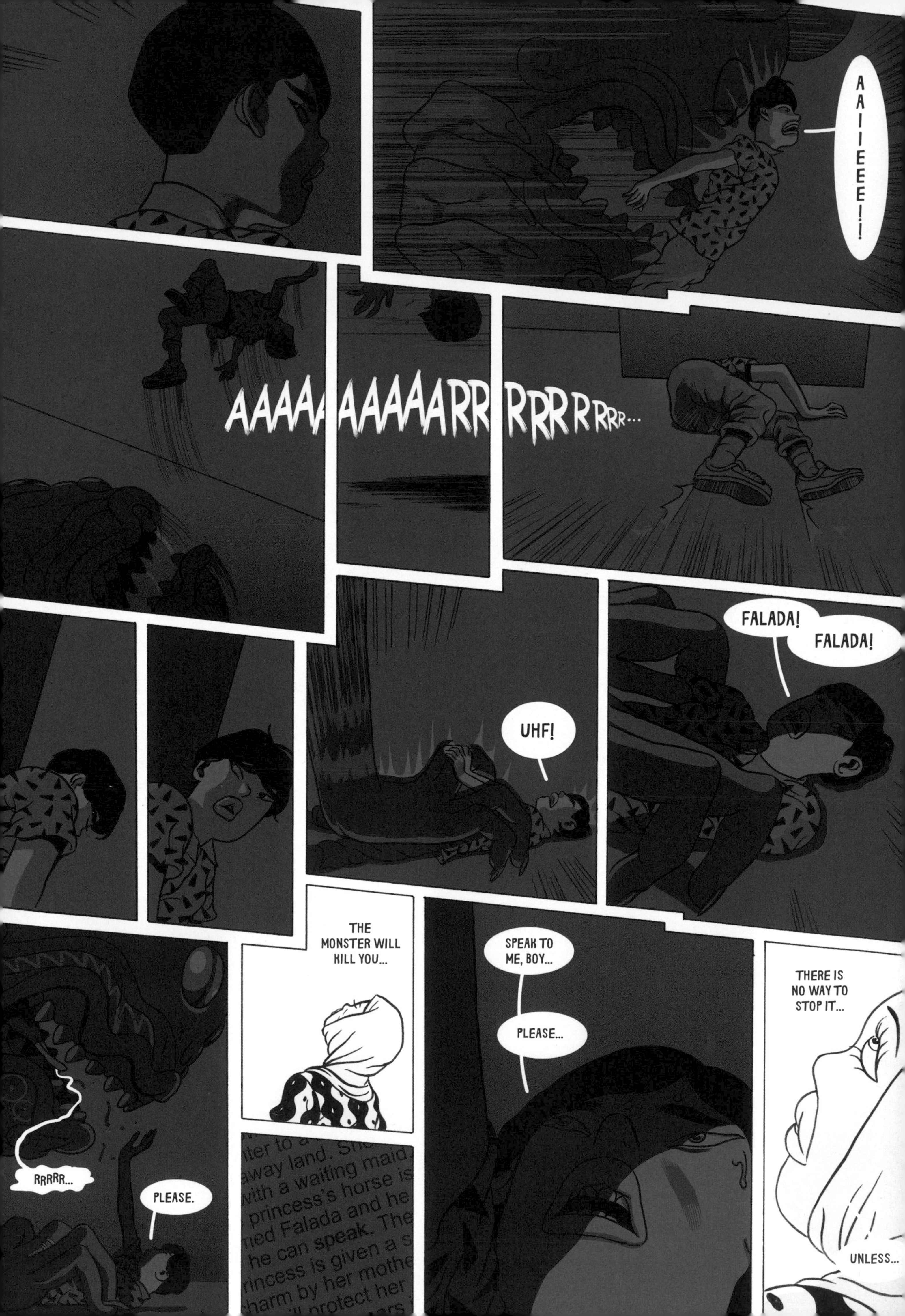

AAIIEEE!!
AAAAAAAAARRRRRRRRR...
UHF!
FALADA!
FALADA!
RRRRR...
PLEASE.
THE MONSTER WILL KILL YOU...
nter to a
away land. She
with a waiting maid.
princess's horse is
med Falada and he
he can speak. The
he can given a
princess is given a
harm by her mothe
SPEAK TO ME, BOY...
PLEASE...
THERE IS NO WAY TO STOP IT...
UNLESS...

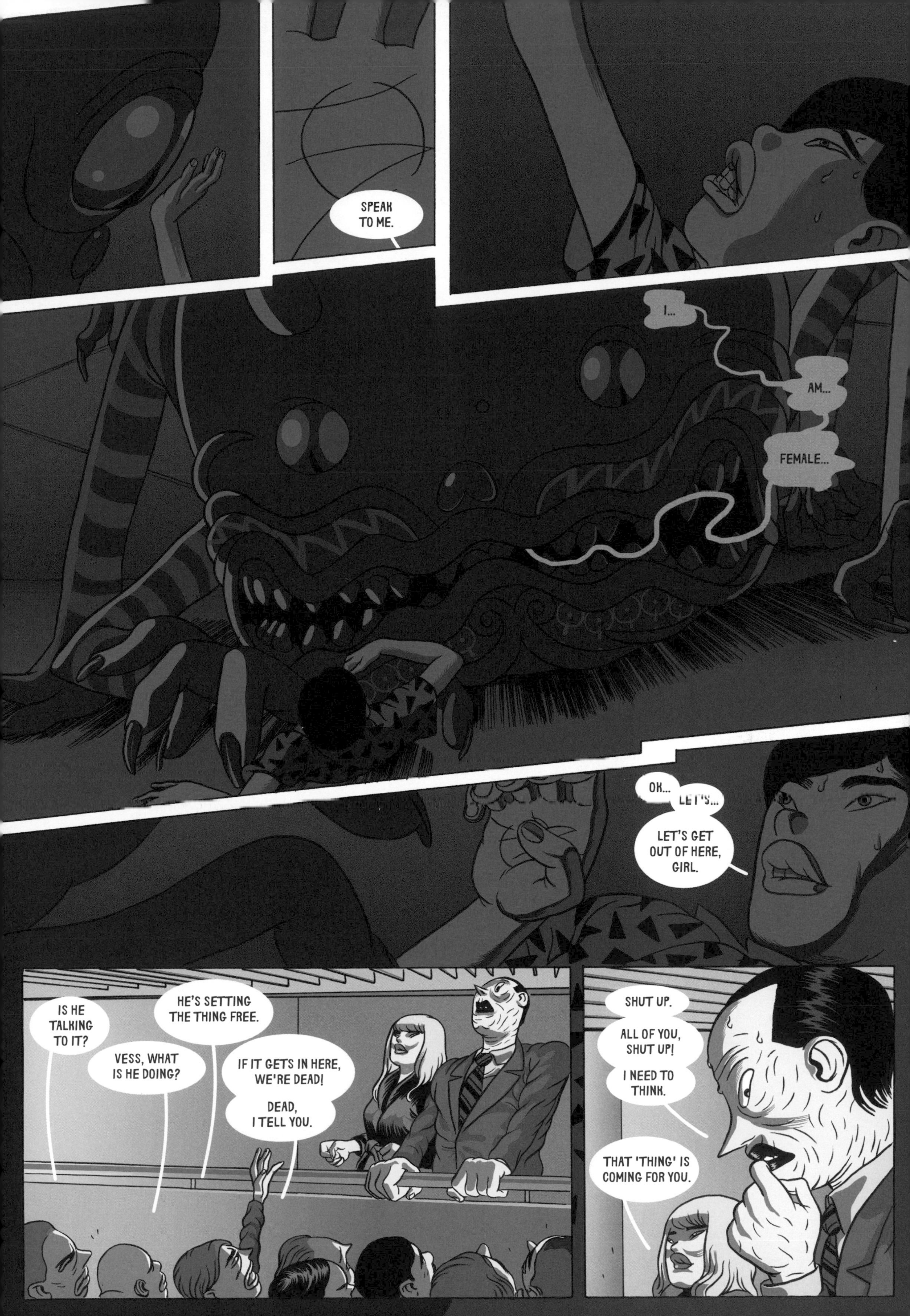
SPEAK TO ME.
I...
AM...
FEMALE...
OK...
LET'S...
LET'S GET OUT OF HERE, GIRL.
IS HE TALKING TO IT?
HE'S SETTING THE THING FREE.
VESS, WHAT IS HE DOING?
IF IT GETS IN HERE, WE'RE DEAD!
DEAD, I TELL YOU.
SHUT UP.
ALL OF YOU, SHUT UP!
I NEED TO THINK.
THAT 'THING' IS COMING FOR YOU.

COME WITH ME IF YOU WANT TO SEE YOUR PET AGAIN!
CONRAD? WHAT ARE YOU—
ROGERS, GET THE CAR READY.
WHERE ARE WE GOING?
FRANCES.
SHE SAID SHE NEEDS TO GET FRANCES.

FRANCES?

CINEM

ROSHAN!

DID YOU JUST WATCH...
THE LINES?
YEA. IT WAS CRAP, RIGHT?

YEAH, PRETTY BAD.

HOW'S YOUR MUM DOING, LOLLY?

WEIRD AS EVER.
HAVEN'T SEEN MUCH OF HER TBH.
I'M NOT SURE THAT SHE'S HAPPY TO HAVE ME BACK, REALLY.

THINK YOUR NEW FRIENDS WANT A WORD, ROSHAN.

WE'RE GOING OVER TO THE SQUARE. YOU COMING?
YEA.
GIMME ONE SECOND.

IT WAS GOOD TO SEE YOU.
BOTH OF YOU.
YOU TOO, MAN.
GIMME A BELL.

YOU CAN KISS HIM IF YOU WANT TO.
MAYBE I WILL.

NEXT TIME.

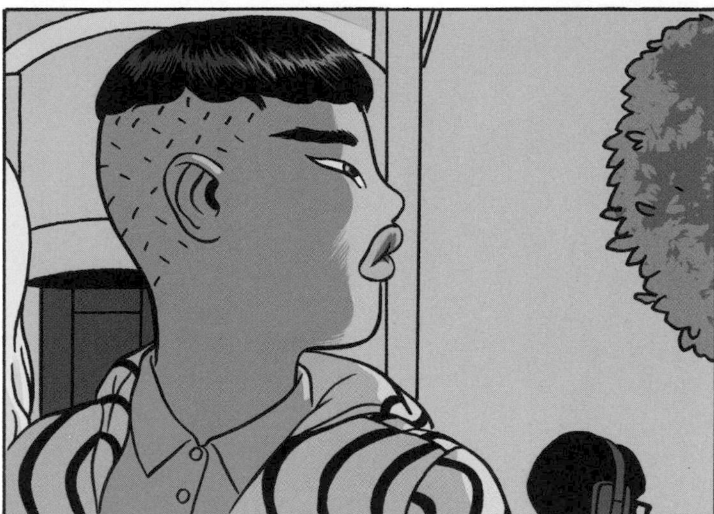

. ...
.. ...
... .

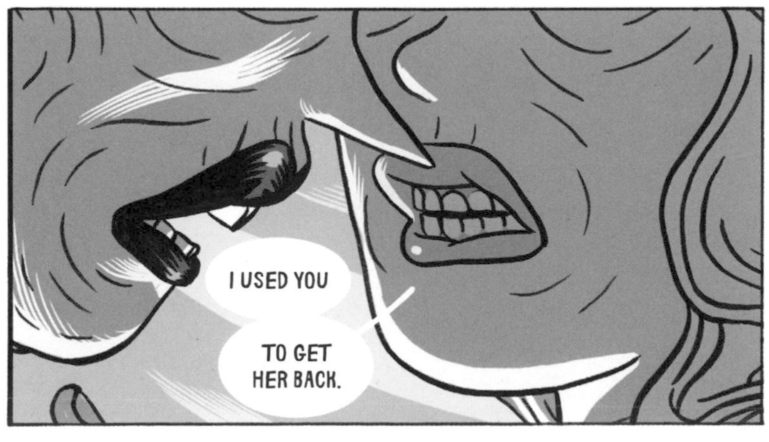
I USED YOU
TO GET HER BACK.

nog
for Roshan
LOOSER
LOOSER
NCE
NCERT
SPECIAL GUEST:
THE TIME
NOV. 19 - FRI. 8:00 P.M.
29.95
SEC ROW SEAT
GEN. ADM.
00008
PRINCE
GEN
NOV.
GC00011
NGUZU NGUZU
7:00pm Monday 30th January
ICA
london
General Admission GIG ONLY
£22.50
Doors at: 7:00pm
£22.50
SIM CONCERTS PRESENT
FRANK OCEAN
PLUS SPECIAL GUESTS
FRIDAY 17 MARCH
DOOR TIME: 18.30
STANDIN TICKET NO: 7148
accompanied by an adult
$5095923
FRIDAY 17
DIAMOND
JAI P